My Feeling Friend

Pam Meyer and Lee Anna Maestas

Fulton Books
Meadville, PA

Published by Fulton Books 2023

ISBN 979-8-88731-207-1 (paperback)
ISBN 979-8-88982-765-8 (hardcover)
ISBN 979-8-88731-208-8 (digital)

Printed in the United States of America

This book is dedicated to Michelle Skinner, who was the inspiration for Daisy Mae. Thank you for always believing in us and cheering us on as we pursue our dreams. This book is also dedicated to our friends and family, who never wavered in their love and support while we chased our dreams.

Author's Note

We are hopeful that you can find solutions to everyday struggles with this book and the Feeling Friend aromatherapy sensory tool. This book was written for everyone, from counselors to kids. While the following story pertains to a younger audience, additional information and resources can be found in the back of the book to help guide your journey.

fear
Anger
Anxiety
Jealousy
Frustration
Sadness
2

My name is Daisy Mae, and I have BIG feelings. My friends say I'm just being dramatic, but my parents say it's OKAY to have big feelings as long as you make good choices.

Sometimes it's really hard! My feelings attack me like little bugs that fly up my nose and won't leave me alone! When those BIG feelings come around, I try to do what Mom always tells me: take a deep breath and count slowly to 10. BUT IT NEVER HELPS! Does this ever happen to you?

Sometimes I get so mad! I feel like a fire-breathing dragon, and I want to burn everything in sight, like when Jimmy knocked over my block tower on purpose and then just laughed. I knew the dragon was coming because my fists got tight, my body got tense, and my face scrunched up. Then the dragon woke up and threw a block at Jimmy as it let loose a great BIG ROAR! What's a dragon supposed to do? That's when I got in trouble, which made me even more upset. I tried to do what Mom always tells me. I took a deep breath and counted slowly to 10. BUT IT NEVER HELPS! Does this ever happen to you?

Other times, I get anxious, and I feel like I can't breathe. It feels like blowing bubbles underwater, but you can't come back up for a new breath of air, like when I got lost at the grocery store and couldn't find my mom. My heart was beating faster and harder until it felt like it was going to explode! My hands got sweaty, and I tried to breathe in. But I couldn't catch my breath. I tried to do what my mom always tells me. I took a deep breath and counted slowly to 10. BUT IT NEVER HELPS! Does this ever happen to you?

I had a BIG feeling yesterday when Dad promised we could play our favorite game. But then his phone rang, and he had to go back to work. Dad promised we would play when he got home. My heart sank into my stomach when he left. My eyes got sad and teary. My throat started to hurt like I swallowed too much food without chewing. Mom tried to comfort me, but I didn't feel like being around anyone or anything, not even Buddy, my dog! As I walked to my room, I tried to do what Mom always tells me. I took a deep breath and counted slowly to 10. BUT IT NEVER HELPS! Does this ever happen to you?

Mom and Dad surprised me with a special present today. I eagerly opened the box and saw the cutest little friend ever! It had great big eyes and fluffy fur. I just had to pick it up! It was so soft on my fingers but crunchy when I squeezed it. It fit perfectly in my hand and was just the right size. It made me feel safe, like when I hold Mom's hand. I already knew I wanted to keep it with me and take it everywhere. When it looked at me, I could just tell it was a friend I could trust and tell my secrets to, just like Mom and Dad. Who makes you feel safe?

Dad said it's called a Feeling Friend, and I can share my BIG feelings with it. Mom said I could put special smells inside my Feeling Friend to help me feel calm and happy when BIG feelings come around and I need help. She said I should give him a special name, so I decided to name him Mr. Snuffers because I use my nose to breathe in the smells that help me feel better. What name would you give to your Feeling Friend?

Then she showed me two bottles of pure essential oils and let me pick my special Feeling Friend smell. The first one, she said, was lavender. I took a deeeeep breath to fill up my nose. All of a sudden, I felt like I was lying in my nana's garden, surrounded by colorful flowers. The flowers were tall, small, skinny, and fat all around me. I could feel the thick green grass tickling my legs and the warmth of the sun on my face. I could hear the quiet whisper of the wind as it blew gently through the flowers and the low buzzing sound of bugs flying from flower to flower. I loved the smell of lavender. It made me feel calm and relaxed. It helped me breathe deeper and slower too, like when you smell a pretty flower. What does lavender make you think of and feel like when you smell it?

Then she let me smell the next bottle; it was orange this time. Again, I took a deeeeep breath to fill up my nose. It made me think of eating fresh, juicy orange slices on a hot day. I could taste the sweet wet orange squishing out of the slice as I took a big bite. I could feel the sticky juice running down my chin and cheeks. I smiled as I felt Mom tickling me as she wiped the stickiness off my face and hands. It made me feel happy and giggly! I was suddenly smiling from ear to ear so hard my cheeks began to hurt, and I wanted to run around the whole neighborhood! What does orange make you think of and feel like when you smell it?

I really loved the way both smells made me feel, and I couldn't wait to try each smell with my Feeling Friend.

Dad asked me, "Are you ready to see how Mr. Snuffers can help you with your BIG feelings?"

I smiled and said "YES!"

He asked me what smell I liked best. I chose orange because it smelled really good! Dad put the essential oil inside Mr. Snuffers and told me to squeeze him tight a few times until I could smell the orange. Then he told me to hold him up to my face and take a deep breath in through my nose while he counted to 4. "Breathe in, 1, 2, 3, 4." I held my deep breath inside my body while Dad counted to 4 again. "Hold it, 1, 2, 3, 4." Then I slowly blew the breath out of my mouth while Dad counted to 4. "Breathe out, 1, 2, 3, 4." We did this four times.

Let's practice: pause and practice the 4-Breath strategy here.

Then Dad asked me to think of a time when I felt happy and safe. I thought for a moment then asked, "Hmm, like when we all went to the park?"

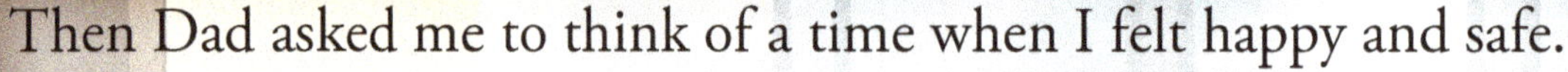

Dad said, "Exactly! Tell me about that day."

I closed my eyes and thought again. I could see a picture clearly in my mind like I was watching a movie. I told him, "It was a hot and sunny day. I had to wear a hat and sunglasses because the sun was so bright it was hard to see. I was excited because you and I ran around in the grass, and we rolled down the hill until I got too dizzy. Then we played in the playground. You pushed me on the swings higher and higher, then you ran underneath the swing until I was flying with the birds! I felt safe and happy. Mom even brought some food for the ducks at the pond.

This is one of my favorite things to do because when my brother gets excited, he squeals like a pig, and it makes me laugh! When I got tired. You got me a snow cone, and then we went home."

Dad smiled and said, "I remember that day too. It was a great day! Do you remember how you felt? Thinking about that fun day, can you feel that now?"

I looked at Mom and Dad then said yes while remembering my happy thought. Mom said we needed to practice remembering my happy thoughts with Mr. Snuffers and the smell. She said that when I have BIG feelings, it's OKAY to feel that way but that Mr. Snuffers and the aroma can help bring back that calm and safe feeling. This way, the smell and Mr. Snuffers can help me remember how to make good choices when those BIG feelings come around.

Let's practice: pause and talk through the visualization now.

It wasn't long before Mr. Snuffers helped me deal with my BIG feelings. Once I was calm and felt safe, I could talk to Mom and Dad about why those BIG feelings came around. This is my favorite part because Mom and Dad never make me feel bad about having BIG feelings. They help me understand why I had a BIG feeling, and then we practice the four-breath strategy with Mr. Snuffers and the smell I like. Mr. Snuffers really helped save the day. IT REALLY HELPS! How has your Feeling Friend helped you?

The End

Limbic System and Olfaction

The limbic system is the part of the brain that oversees our behavioral and emotional responses. The hypothalamus, the amygdala, the thalamus, and the hippocampus make up the limbic system. Together they are responsible for three main functions: memory storage and retrieval, regulating emotional states, and autonomic responses, which includes the "fight or flight" response. The olfactory bulb, a person's sense of smell, has over one thousand receptors. It is next door to the limbic system and therefore has a direct connection or pathway to the limbic system in the brain. For this reason, the sense of smell has the strongest link to the recall of memories and emotional states both consciously or unconsciously. This is how the Feeling Friend tool and the aromatherapy inside can help navigate and regulate emotional states—by recalling positive memories and emotions. Practicing the strategies while a child is feeling happy and safe is important to help establish and reinforce the scent association.

Essential Oils

Essential oils are volatile chemical compounds derived from plants. Essential oil plant extracts have been used for centuries in many cultures around the world for a variety of health and medicinal benefits. Just like plants, essential oils can have a variety of effects. Some essential oils can promote soothing, toning, and grounding feelings while others can promote energizing, warming, and renewing feelings. Lavender can help promote feelings of calm, comfort, and restfulness. Orange or citrus oils can help promote energizing, renewing, and uplifting feelings. Any pure essential oil can be used with the Feeling Friend aromatherapy sensory tool.

4-Breath Strategy

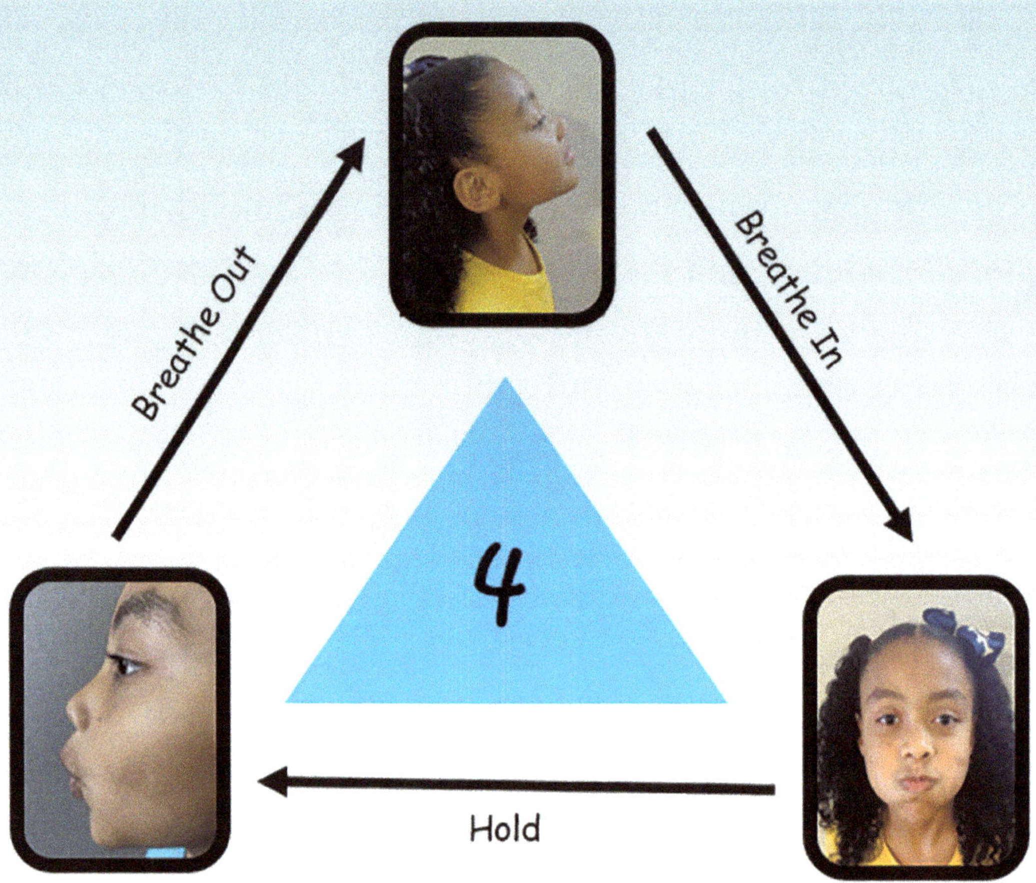

Visualization
Happy Thought

Visualization is the formation of a mental image. When helping a child visualize, it helps to have them close their eyes and create a picture in their mind. Have the child describe as many details as possible. This may require you to ask probing questions using the five senses—for example, "What do you see, hear, touch, and smell?" "Was it a hot day?" and "What were you wearing?" Toward the end of the visualization, ask the child, "How were you feeling? Can you feel that now?" If a child does not have a happy, safe memory to recall, help them create one.

Validate and Process Feelings

When a child is emotionally escalated, it is important to validate their feelings in the moment. For example, if a child is throwing a temper tantrum, let them know it is okay to feel upset. This can be done with verbal statements such as "It seems like you are upset about this." Validation is a brief acknowledgement of what they are experiencing in the moment. This is an important first step because it lets the child know their feelings are valid and can sometimes help initiate the de-escalation process. In addition, validation can help create a safe space for a child to navigate their emotions. After the validation is a great time to utilize the Feeling Friend tool and strategies.

Once the child is calm, it is important to process what happened with a trusted adult. For example, after a child has had a temper tantrum, ask for their permission to discuss what happened together. If they are ready, you can ask probing questions about what happened or triggered the upset. This can help you and the child identify potential triggers that may occur in the future. After this, discuss what calm-down strategies worked for both you and the child. This conversation should also include how the child felt while emotionally escalated. Ask, "How did you know you were getting mad, sad, anxious, etc.?" and "Where did you feel it in your body?" Having your child identify where they are feeling tense or uneasy can help them learn to self-identify when they may need their Feeling Friend. This can help empower a child to help themselves in selecting tools and strategies to calm and comfort themselves in the moment.

Resources

Feeling Friend YouTube channel (www.youtube.com/c/feelingfriend)

The Feeling Friend YouTube channel has each of the strategies in this book modeled with a child and teen. There are many additional videos with strategies that may help a child in need as well as resources for adult facilitators.

Where to purchase a Feeling Friend (www.feelingfriend.com)

We recommend having a at least two Feeling Friends for each user. The full-size and mini are a great combination as they each provide different tactile sensory inputs. Having multiple Feeling Friends on hand allows the user to keep one in a central location or "home base" and another for on-the-go use.

Contact Feeling Friend at feelingfriendsllc@gmail.com

Are you a mental health agency, educator, or health provider? Feeling Friend would like to offer you training with your bulk order. Trainings are a great way to provide hands-on professional development for a variety of strategies with the Feeling Friend aromatherapy sensory tool. Trainings also provide more in-depth understanding of aromatherapy and essential oils. Contact us directly to inquire about the training and purchasing options.

This book code entitles you to a discount on the purchase of a Feeling Friend of your choice on our website. Visit www.feelingfriend.com to order your Feeling Friend today!

Book Code:

FF02142020

About the Authors

Pam Meyer is a Licensed Professional Counselor of twenty-two years and is currently working as an elementary school counselor. She has an MEd in community counseling. Pam has extensive experience working with treatment foster families and outpatient therapy with children and adolescents. She currently lives in New Mexico with her husband, two daughters, and two dogs.

Lee Anna Maestas is an early childhood educator of nine years and is currently working as a kindergarten teacher. She has a BS in early childhood multicultural education (B-3) and an MA in language, literacy, and sociocultural studies. Lee Anna has also worked with behavior management in young children and children who have experienced trauma or emotional disturbance. She currently lives in New Mexico with her husband and three dogs.

Pam and Lee Anna first met as coworkers in a local elementary school where they put their heads together to find a child-friendly way of introducing the benefits of aromatherapy with the children in their community. This is how the Feeling Friend aromatherapy sensory tool was created. Both Pam and Lee Anna wanted to help empower parents, kids, and professionals alike to have tools and strategies that work for children of all backgrounds and experiences. Writing this book has been a lifelong dream of Pam's and a great support for teaching children healthy coping strategies.